Book Endorsements for

CULTIVATE:
Tailgate Huddles to Grow Stronger Teams

Jeff has an amazing gift to write, lead and inspire passion in people who work in the green industry. *Cultivate* will impassion you to instill and cultivate a winning team in any organization!

Michael J. DeBoer
Landscape & Grounds Manager
Aquinas College, Grand Rapids, Michigan

Cultivate is a gem for all team managers and crew leaders in any industry. Using the short stories and thought-provoking questions provided in the book, your investment in just a few minutes of conversation can create more cohesive and cooperative crews and result in enduring positive culture change. This book makes it easy to read, lead, and succeed.

Jennifer Gulick
Principal, Urban Canopy Works LLC
Certified Arborist; Certified Forester

In *Cultivate*, Jeff hits the nail on the head again. Each one of these huddles are exactly the real-life scenarios that we encounter as managers. When we see that others have our same issues, it reassures us that we are on the right track, not only for our improvement but also for all of those that we direct.

Kim A. Byram
University of Alabama
Associate Manager, Facilities and Grounds

Prestigious national awards and over thirty years' experience at the highest levels of landscape management give Jeff McManus an incredible insight into developing leadership, team building, team motivation, and company culture. In his book, Jeff has been able to reduce complex management concepts into easy-to-understand-and-apply stories that will benefit everyone from the beginning crewmember up to senior management.

Harry Ponder
Professor Emeritus
Auburn University

Cultivate is a great follow-up to *Growing Weeders into Leaders*. In a fifteen-minute session, key management words are defined and used in an everyday example. These parables of everyday life in the horticultural world can be adapted to many different fields of work. I can see this becoming a great training tool to encourage cooperation and communication within a workforce.

Roger L. Conner, CGM
ISA Certified Arborist
Superintendent Tree Management
Landscape Services

Jeff McManus has crafted a masterful mix of stories, quotes and practical advice in this timely book, *Cultivate: A Landscape Leaders Guide to Empowering Teams*. There is something for everyone in these pages, whether you're just starting your career or are a seasoned veteran. If you're looking for ways to improve yourself and your team, this is it.

Anthony L. Williams, CGCS, CGM
Director of Golf Course & Landscape Operations
TPC Four Seasons Resort and Club Dallas at Las Colinas

I honestly believe that as you read through this book and share it in small groups, beneficial discussions will happen that will help in building a stronger group of team members willing to excel as service providers of choice. Each little story serves as a guidepost to create a productive group discussion on how to succeed as a person. It's definitely a tool worth having and sharing.

Gerald "Gerry" S. Dobbs, CGM
Grounds Manager
University of Texas at El Paso

What I admire about Jeff McManus is that he has accomplished what he authors. And now, in a clever twist with *Cultivate*, Jeff brings together 31 short stories that, when woven together, become an easy-to-implement and practical tool for developing individuals and growing a great team. Every business can easily implement the *Cultivate* strategy and create an interactive environment where individuals can comfortably participate and embrace personal and team growth. If you've met Jeff, you know he is genuinely committed to inspiring and motivating individuals to accomplish team success. After reading this book and embracing this as a tool, you'll quickly conclude that, "it is a time to create trust with team members by respecting their input and listening. They will, for the first time, hear themselves embrace the concepts as a team."

Tom Ewing
Landscape Program Development
Proven Winners

Cultivate shares some very coachable moments to make a leader out of someone in many different circumstances. This book is an insightful read and can help others in similar work situations better themselves and their team.

Amanda Klenke
Horticulturist
Ole Miss Landscape Services

Every organization is doing something right or it would disintegrate. Jeff's passion to pull together the right stuff and make it easy to read and quickly adaptable is becoming legendary to those of us close to him. Looking for a competitive edge? Here it is.

Fred Fellner, Ph.D.
Landscape Department Head
Louisiana State University

Cultivate: Tailgate Huddles to Grow Stronger Teams offers excellent talking points to start conversations within our team so we can become closer and more cohesive. This is a book our entire department will use as a tool in our team meetings.

Michael Gildea
Garden and Grounds Manager
Top 10 U.S. Platinum Club (Maryland)

Our company has had the privilege of working alongside Jeff during company retreats, and we have seen firsthand the effects of his leadership training. We are excited that *Cultivate* will be an integral tool within our team and training new team members. It is a true gift to have Jeff and his motivation and leadership skills, but it is a rare find to partner with someone who is in the same industry that understands who we are and where we are trying to go as a company.

Gerrick Taylor
Owner-Taylor's Landscape Supply & Nursery
Bluffton, SC

The thirty-one attributes listed in *Cultivate* go well beyond the landscape, green industry. These values can be applied in any team atmosphere that is striving for success or in need of a change (personally or professionally). These thirty-one core concepts will challenge YOU as a leader but, more importantly, will help lay the foundation for nurturing positive growth, enhancing communication and creating leadership opportunities within your organization.

Eric Harshman
Grounds Superintendent
Transylvania University

As leaders, we should influence, motivate and enable our employees to not only be better employees, but better people. Jeff's book gives us the tools to cultivate your team and help them reach their full potential. This book may be marketed to the green industry, but its lessons apply to all lines of work.

Brett Ganas—RLA, CEFP
Director—Grounds, Sanitation and Fleet Management
Facilities Management Division
University of Georgia

Like *Growing Weeders into Leaders*, Jeff again offers a well-written, easy-to-understand book I can hand to any of my employees or co-workers, confident that each of them will find something that speaks directly to them, either reaffirming an already positive work ethic or gently nudging them in a slightly different direction from where they may have been headed.

David Love
Director, Landscaping and Grounds /Sports Turf /Sustainability
Longwood University

Jeff is more than a grower of plants. He grows himself as well as all those around him. Attaining new vision and inspired attitude is only a portion of what he encourages and exemplifies to not only his co-workers, but anyone that he encounters. I consider it an honor to not only be his friend, but also his brother in Christ. Jeff devotes himself to improving himself and others. Don't miss an opportunity to be challenged and blessed and grow as an individual and team. Get your copy and share it with others, and let's all grow together. It's not red and blue or maroon and white. It's simply being a better you.

Bart Prather
Associate Director, Campus Landscape (Retired)
Mississippi State University

Jeff McManus is a great leader among men. His mentorship has brought me the wealth of a hard-working crew and the respect of my leaders. In this book, *Cultivate,* Jeff brings to life realistic scenarios. He shares the insight of problem-solving and leading. Jeff allows us to put ourselves into any of the situations and play them out in our minds to understand how we might react or work through the possibilities of everyday life circumstances. Thank you again, Jeff. I can never thank you enough.

Jimmy Viars CGM, CBLP
Grounds Manager
Gloucester County Public Schools

In reading through the *Cultivate* team exercises, I was reminded how important it is to encourage open communication with your staff and solicit honest feedback for the work they perform. Everyone wants to know that their input and opinion matters and this concise, to the point "tailgate" approach provides a hands-on format for successful team building. A must read for managers and supervisors who need a fresh look at getting back to the basic caring and sharing principles.

Mark Feist
American University
Assistant Director of Facilities Operations (Retired)
President, Professional Grounds Management Society

Cultivate is about creating dynamic teams as well as creating trust. This book uses practical, relatable examples that many in the green industry have indeed experienced firsthand. The thoughtful creation of each chapter focuses on breaking down different soft skill elements to help you and your team begin the conversation about teamwork, trust and how the team could grow together. I highly recommend this book to all in the pursuit of evolving your team into a dynamic, positive, and super productive one!

Paula Sliefert
Senior Marketing Manager
The Toro Co.

Cultivate, with its quick discussion modules, is the perfect tool for your leadership toolbox! The discussions with leaders can be short or expanded on as time permits, but they keep these important principles fresh in your team's minds. This is a simple, effective way to build a leadership foundation with the "boots on the ground" supervisors.

Sandra Obenour-Dowd
Grounds Superintendent
University of Arizona

Cultivate: Tailgate Huddles to Grow Stronger Teams is a must-read for leaders in the green industry, or frankly any industry, who seek to further develop their leadership skills. The author presents excellent hypothetical scenarios and challenges the reader to proactively develop solutions on their own. This book will undoubtedly serve those in leadership or even lead positions to better themselves and all of those they work with. Raising each other up for excellence is the mainstay goal of this book! I'm extra motivated about sharpening my own leadership abilities and skills after reading this book. Another fantastic read by Jeff McManus!

Bruce DeVrou, CGM
Facilities Project Manager
VP—PGMS 2021 Executive Board

I just wanted to read a few of the topics, but ended up reading the entire book in one sitting. This book is the daily devotional to leadership excellence. From the Table of Contents to the last printed words are invaluable topics that will engage and inspire employees to build teamwork, relationships, and leadership characteristics. This book will become a foundation upon which to build leadership excellence within any department. *Cultivate* is the "painting of the Golden Gate Bridge"; once you are finished with it, it's time to start over and begin again reasserting these leadership quality topics. The missing link to daily leadership affirmations and team building—found.

Justin Sutton
Director, Landscape Services
Auburn University

Highly recommended! Jeff will map out a course from five methods of ideal leadership vision, courage, integrity, humility, and strategic planning. His work and passion for leadership will rejuvenate your team performance and personality with a professional outcome.

Kevin Scott Mercer CGM, CSFM, LICM, MGC
Grounds & Landscape Manger
Denison University

For most of us going to work, you have a set of tools you use to perform that job. *Cultivate* is exactly that, a tool for you to use to help build and maintain your team. Even better, it's a tool that works for anyone that manages people, not just those in the green industry. Jeff's *Cultivate* gives examples of real situations about the hardest and most rewarding part of your job, managing your team.

Joe Kovolyan, CGM, CSFM
President-Elect, Professional Grounds Management Society

As I read Jeff's book, *Cultivate*, I was immediately searching my team and myself for all of the thirty-one qualities, and how we can apply them to be better employees and leaders, ultimately providing *THE BEST* customer service!

> Donna Hibbs
> VP of Grounds and Landscaping
> Masonic Homes Kentucky

The Lord works in mysterious ways! I've known Jeff for 30-plus years, and I know him to be a man of faith, so I guess I should expect this from Jeff. As we were planning out our team meetings for the balance of the year, we contemplated the content, and I was searching for meaningful ways to engage our staff. Then, like a gift from above, Jeff asked me to read the manuscript for his new book, and it was all there. Many thanks to Jeff for his insights in *Cultivate,* and for giving me a powerful tool to grow my team and company.

> Steve Stanford
> President
> Plantz.com

I see this book as a tremendous tool to be used by both the new and the seasoned leader. These targeted talking points are extremely relatable to every team in ANY type of work. Jeff has used his landscape canvas to paint a phenomenal painting for all to observe and appreciate. Using these topics as a launch pad for guided discussions with your team is a great way to engage team members, gain trust, and "cultivate" an environment for team growth. Love this book!

> Mark Davis
> Major, United States Marine Corps (Retired)

Cultivate is all about cultivating thirty-one winning qualities into your team and is a tool that every business can incorporate into their training program. Developing individuals into a well-oiled, cohesive group of team players starts with each valuing themselves, respecting others, taking pride in their work and taking ownership for their attitudes and actions. Leading by example comes to mind when thinking of Jeff McManus and what he has done with his team at Ole Miss. Jeff has a masterful way of presenting these concepts in short, concise training opportunities. Can't wait to include these tailgate huddles into our training program.

Martha G. Hill, RLA
General Manager
Earthscape Supply, LLC

CULTIVATE

Tailgate Huddles to Grow Stronger Teams

THREE STEPS FOR BUILDING STRONGER
TEAM PLAYERS, GETTING GREATER RESULTS,
AND DEVELOPING TEAM UNITY

JEFF McMANUS

Published The Jeff McManus Group
Illustrations Beth Robinson
Cover Design by FormattedBooks
Front cover photo Mallory McManus—Mvisuals.info

ISBN: XXXXXXXXXXXX

DEDICATION

This book is dedicated to all the landscape, spray
tech, irrigation, sports turf, parks, tree arborist,
golf course, and all grounds staff who work daily
behind the scenes to create beautiful and aesthetically
pleasing grounds that inspire the world.

CONTENTS

FOREWORD

Business leadership books offer plenty of advice on how to improve performance and productivity, increase employee engagement, and even have success in life. Many promise outcomes of riches and glory through their own methods of dressed-up common sense. This book is different.

Jeff and I have grown our friendship since being introduced by our mutual mentor and professor, Dr. Harry Ponder, several years ago. Jeff's unique ability to paint a real-world picture of how to grow and lead people from the ground level is what makes his approach so appealing. The fact that his methodology has been tested and proven on the grounds of one of nation's most coveted campuses while achieving world-class recognition is no coincidence.

Landscape horticulture is all about serving the needs of others. Accomplishment comes when we make our client's image the best possible and brand success is first associated with the landscape. Attractive color, good order, separation, and crisp detail where it matters. Well-trained staff who see solutions and are wired to "own it" are the secret sauce. This does not happen without intentional and caring leadership. Jeff gets it. He sees the potential and value of each person on his team, patiently paints the vision, and then steps back and lets them grow. It is a beautiful process.

In the beginning, I thought growing a business was only about selling $20M worth of work. This process is so much more valuable than that. This book is a living example of daily short stories celebrating the small steps that build values and character within people (the secret sauce). We are made to be in nature and in community. Jeff and I both see the landscape as the perfect mission for celebrating people and place, and when done well, a most worthy investment.

Our company has been practicing the daily "tailgate huddles" for years and we have found it to be the best place for reinforcing, training, and sharing vision and values of the company. With the release of this book, we have a very practical guide, backed by real-world events to help elevate the new standard. It is my hope that you find this collection of stories and lessons encouraging for you and your team. I have heard Jeff says numerous times, "If we are going to do a job, let's be the absolute best." Winning what he refers to as "National Championships" is no accident. It takes patience, discipline, and a caring vision for the most important part of the business, our people.

Tony Gibson
CEO
Gibson Landscape
Atlanta, Georgia

INTRODUCTION

In the landscape industry, we face an ever-changing host of challenges, such as labor shortages, weather, unreal client expectations, budget challenges, and growth opportunities. It is the leader who constantly grows and adapts to the changes who will experience the outcomes he or she dreams about.

The smart way to increase your production and reduce costly delays is to invest in the people you hire. Great leaders know that they cannot carry the burden of doing the work, growing the organization, and exceeding the customers' expectations. It takes great people working together if you want to continue to reach the next level.

Just like plants, people need an environment that is conducive to healthy growth and fruit production. Before we plant our first plant, we develop a design that is our road map for the project. We cultivate the soil, check the drainage, and add soil conditioner. We give our plants every opportunity to grow and be healthy and successful. Hopefully, over time, those new plants will be watered and fed and get the right amount of sunlight. If we have a maintenance contract on our new plants, we have a twelve-month plan that may include measures to prevent weeds, remove weeds, fertilize, monitor for pests, add mulch, and even prune.

We hire our teams and hope the individual members are good people, and we send them out to do the work. We rely on our seasoned staff to train and coach them in the skills and attitudes they need to succeed.

I did it like this for years. It works to some degree, but little did I know I was missing a great opportunity for growth, both for myself and, more importantly, for them. I began to wonder how could I empower my people to be great landscapers who can solve problems, stop employee drama, and be passionate about being the best of the best.

This book is a tool to invest in yourself and your team. As you gather to discuss priorities for the day or huddle after lunch or maybe even at the end of the day, take two minutes to *Cultivate* your team. I suggest you read each page ahead of time and, if you can, read it out loud to practice. When you read it to the team, take your time to allow everyone to consider the message.

The questions at the end are provided to encourage team members to participate in discussions about the word or phrase. It will be awkward the first few times you do it, but trust me, after the third day or so, it becomes a great team builder.

Here is what I found: Most hardworking team members will really appreciate talking about these values; they will, for the first time, hear themselves embrace the concepts as a team. These values slowly will become a part of your organization, and you will see your teams operate at a new level of maturity and purpose. I personally have done this with my teams for more than eight years and have found that the more we engage the values, the better we get and the higher the quality of our results. And, almost as a bonus, the drama has dropped to almost zero.

Just like planting new plants, this exercise needs more attention as you get started. The goal is to get two or three people engaged in discussing the questions. If your team is not a vocal bunch, you may need to "seed" the discussion by pulling out a couple of team leaders ahead of time and getting them to help start the discussions.

This is not a time to jump on a soapbox about policies or pet peeves. It is a time to create trust by respecting team members' input, listening, and encouraging them.

Watch the growth; it happens slowly. I am excited to hear what happens with your team. In time, you will reap a reward. Go and plant the seeds of greatness in your culture.

After you do a few pages with your team, I would be honored to hear from you. You can email me jeff@jeffmcmanus.com or call me on my cellphone at 662-832-5678 and let me know what happens.

Jeff McManus

INSTRUCTIONS ON HOW TO USE THIS BOOK

THREE STEPS FOR BUILDING STRONGER TEAMS

Step 1:

Read the story ahead of your meeting with the team. I find that small groups of seven-to-twelve people works best. The definitions are from my thoughts and experience, not necessarily out of a dictionary.

Let each person in the group answer a short ice breaker question before you read. I usually do something like this. "Tell us your name, how long you have worked here and what is your favorite food or who is your favorite athlete?"

Explain to the team that this is a time of trust and encourage them to respect one another's ideas and comments.

Step 2:

Read the page aloud to the team.

Step 3:

Ask the questions and allow time for people to answer. It may be silent at first, but give it time. Feel free to add your own questions for the group.

The goal is to start conversations and let your team hear themselves share in the lessons.

It is up to you how long you want to discuss.

Through the discussions, your team will grow in their thinking and idea ownership.

After you do a few pages with your team, I would be honored to hear from you. You can email me jeff@jeffmcmanus.com or call me on my cellphone at 662-832-5678 and let me know what happens.

Have fun!

ADAPTABLE

Defined:

Flexible, able to adjust, and move forward.

Kenny's team was able to adapt and overcome many obstacles to meet their customer's sod deadline.

Quote:

"You don't drown by falling in the water; you drown by staying there."—Edwin Louis Cole, author and founder of the Christian Men's Network

Story:

Being adaptable is one of the top qualities that people who work outdoors are known for. Oftentimes when teams are working on normal maintenance schedules, they get an unexpected request, or maybe the weather changes. Kenny and his team were about halfway finished laying sod for a last-minute, urgent project for a client. The client's septic tank had been replaced, and she had a dinner event coming up that very night. Kenny's crew showed up, prepped the large area, and started putting in fresh sod. Before long, the cloudy skies above opened up with a gentle, cool spring shower that showed no signs of letting up.

Kenny and the team never stopped. They kept a positive attitude as they said, "Let's finish." Since there was no thunder or lightning, they kept laying the sod and finished the job before the ground became too saturated. Later, Kenny's boss thanked him and the crew for getting the job done, saying, "You overcame the weather and finished." Kenny smiled and walked to his truck, saying, "That is who we are; we are known for being able to adapt and overcome problems."

The next day, Kenny's boss got a call from an excited client who had seen the crew finishing up their work in the rain. "You have some of the best employees in the world," she said. "I can't tell you how much it means to me that you finished my yard, even with the rain. My event was a big success and nobody ever suspected what kind of shape my yard was in just a few hours earlier. It came together beautifully because your team adapted and overcame the short deadline and the rain. Thank you!"

Questions:

What challenges did Kenny and his team overcome to get the job completed on time?

How could Kenny and the team have responded negatively to the obstacles?

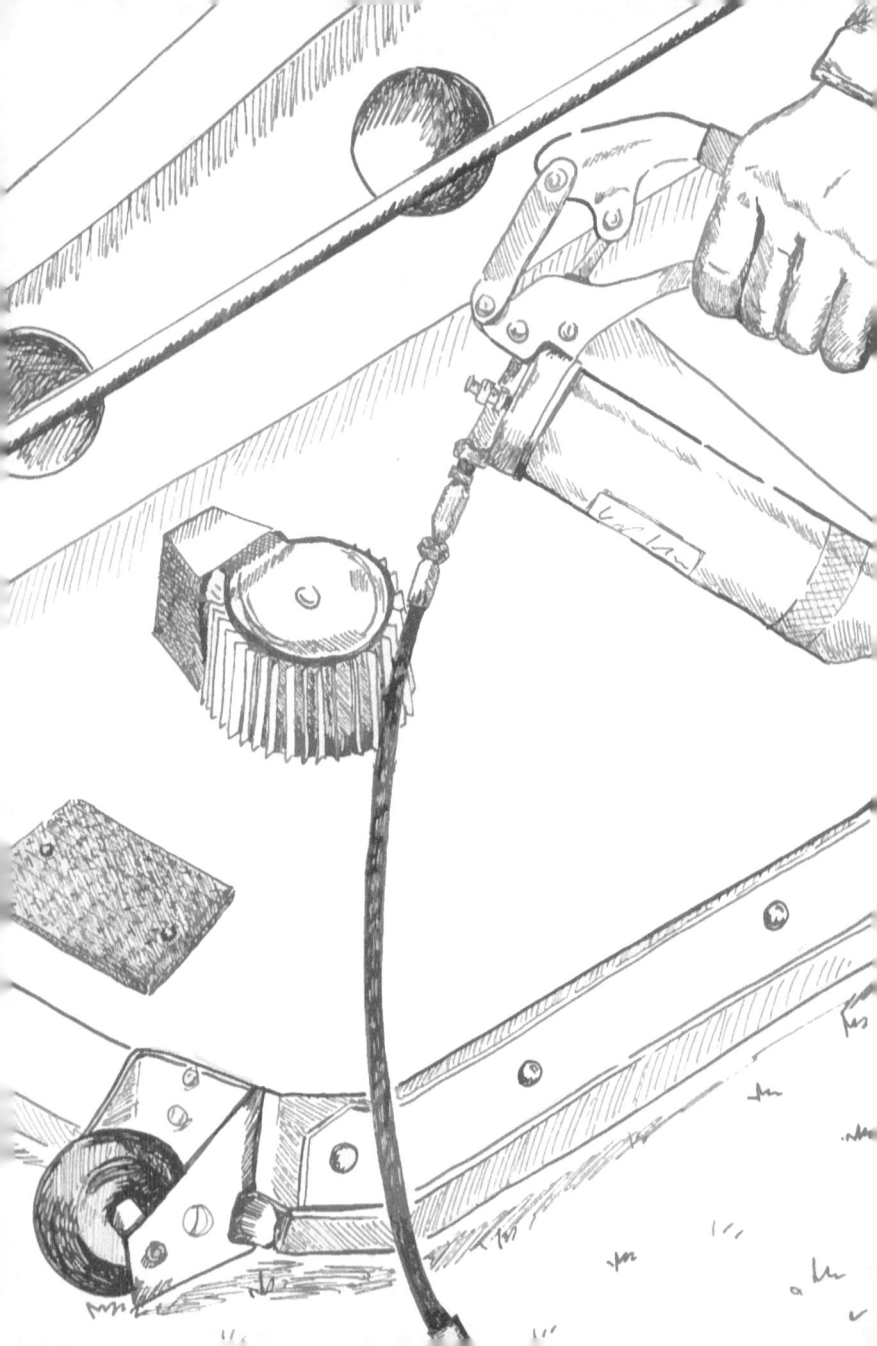

ATTITUDE

Defined:

A person's mental and emotional mood.

The landscape crew likes working with Pete, the mechanic, because he is always in a good mood and willing to help others.

Quote:

"The greatest day in your life and mine is when we take total responsibility for our attitudes. That's the day we truly grow up."—John C. Maxwell, New York Times-bestselling leadership author and minister

Story:

At work, Dustin walked past Pete, who was wearing a big grin as he leaned over a mower. "Hey Pete, you seem to really like doing what you do," Dustin said. "You're in a good mood every day—why is that?"

Pete stopped greasing the mower, stood up, and looked Dustin in the eye. "The first time I worked here three years ago, I acted like a spoiled brat," he explained. "I complained, I moaned, I criticized and grumbled almost every day. I kept thinking everybody owed me something. So, I quit here and went to work across town pouring concrete, making really good money. But I had the same stinking attitude I had before.

"I met a man there who took an interest in me; his name was Gus. He pulled me aside and gave me some straight-up good advice. He let me know where my bad attitude was leading me, but I didn't listen to him; I thought I knew it all. After about six months, the company had had enough. My bad attitude had to improve or I'd need to find another place to work. Well, my pride got in the way, and I walked out.

"But the economy was bad and I couldn't find work. My wife had just had our first baby, the bills were piling up, and I was at my wits' end. So, I swallowed my pride and asked for my old job back here as a mechanic. The boss was pretty hesitant because I wasn't a model employee, but he said I could come back if I was willing to go through a new leadership course they were running. I had no idea what that was but I needed a job, so I agreed. That course actually helped me become aware of some of the wrong mindsets I had about myself, my work, and the people I worked with.

"I figured out after a while that I am responsible for me and my attitude, regardless of what happens. That was the day I grew up. From that day on, I decided I was going to be in charge of my mood every day, no matter what. I choose to be in a good mood every day."

Questions:

Before Pete changed his attitude, what was he like?

What helped Pete change his attitude?

BIG PICTURE

Defined:

Seeing the long-range situation, how the little details affect the overall situation.

Craig was disappointed the team had not gotten to work today because of the rain, but they did accomplish some much-needed team training and equipment maintenance.

Quote:

"Details create the big picture."—Sanford I. Weill, philanthropist and former Citigroup CEO

Story:

Craig's crew didn't understand why they had to go over to the other side of campus, into Jane's zone, to mow; that was not their area to maintain. "We always have to bail Jane's crew out by coming over and mowing their area," one of the crew members complained. "Yeah, and they never have to come to our side of campus and mow," another chimed in. Craig just listened as the crew vented and got their frustrations off their chests.

After everybody cooled down, Craig explained the full scope of the situation. "I understand your frustrations and how you might at first believe we're getting the short end of the stick, so to speak. But let me ask you to stop for second and look at the campus from our customers' perspective. When prospective students and their parents come onto campus, they don't care who mows where; they don't know the campus is in zones for our convenience. They see the whole campus as one place.

"In reality, the campus mowing is all of our responsibility. Every bit of it. We divide the campus into zones to help us manage it, not to create walls or boundaries that were not meant to be crossed. Oh, and since Jane's crew has a lot more turf than we do, it will be normal for us to go over from time to time and help mow in their zone.

"In the big picture, we are all responsible for the beauty and maintenance of the entire campus, not just our zones."

Questions:

Why was Craig's crew so negative about mowing in Jane's zone?

What was really the big picture Craig's crew needed to see about the campus?

BLIND SPOT

Defined:

An area of your life you cannot see.

Mario had a blind spot in his life that he did not see, but fortunately, someone cared enough to show him.

Quote:

"Ego creates blind spots."—Eric Schmidt, former Google CEO

Story:

When Mario, a respected leader, was asked to give an update at the weekly meeting, you could see his body language change, almost as if he became annoyed. After this behavior continued each week, his boss asked him to ride with him to the nursery to get some plants. The two talked a bit and the boss praised Mario for some really positive work he was doing for the company. Then the boss asked Mario if he could share a few observations and a blind spot that was holding him back from being a great leader. Mario was a bit puzzled, but said, "Yes, please share."

The boss shared many positive aspects of Mario and how proud he was of all Mario had accomplished. Later in the drive, he added, "Mario, you are a hard worker, very dependable, and a problem solver. You have lots of leadership potential here with us. Let me share one blind spot you have so you can work on it and go even further in your career. At our weekly meetings, your attitude comes across as negative. People are not sure if you're mad, frustrated, or exactly what is going on with you; it is so out of character for you. Because you are a leader, that behavior hurts your ability to lead."

After a few seconds of silence, Mario replied, "You're right. I don't know why I get frustrated when I'm speaking at the meeting; maybe I feel like we are wasting time when we could be outside working. I get anxious and have lots of work I want to get done." The boss and Mario arrived at the nursery, and the boss said, "I appreciate that you take your responsibility seriously, Mario. That is what makes you a good leader. You remember how unorganized we used to be before we added the short weekly meeting? We were growing, and it was getting crazy trying to see the big picture of our company. By meeting, we increased the communication with everyone." Mario nodded and smiled. "Yes, it was very bad, I had forgotten about the chaos. You'll see a much better attitude from me in the meetings moving forward. Thank you for sharing that blind spot."

Questions:

What was Mario's blind spot?

Why was Mario's blind spot harmful to him and the company?

BUY-IN

Defined:

To commit and participate with your full belief.

I believe my role is significant to help others win. I care and have an attitude that is coachable, an attitude that reflects I want the best for our team, our property, and our organization. I buy in when it is about the team and not about me.

Quote:

"Individual commitment to a group effort—that is what makes a team work, a company work, a society work, a civilization work."—Vince Lombardi, Pro Football Hall of Fame coach and two-time Super Bowl champion

Story:

Pete had been working with the School Grounds Department six months when he first recognized the term "buy-in." He had wondered why their leader, Joe, had been so committed about his work; someone said, "He believes in what he does. Joe is 'bought in.'" This confused Pete, so he asked Joe, "How can you buy in to something you don't own? You don't own this business; you are an employee. We're here to do our time, get a paycheck, and one day we retire and get a pension. I don't get why you care so much about the work."

Joe was glad Pete asked such a good question. He answered, "Buy-in is a belief in something. Some people buy in to being sports fans and love their teams, root for them, but they don't own them. But they still feel they are a part of that team, based on their beliefs. It is the same at work: I can buy in with my attitude by wanting my organization to be successful, do my part in helping them be successful, and show it in my actions. Whether it is a sports team or work, my attitude is the key to buying in. If I don't buy in or believe in what I am doing is important, I tend to not participate with as much energy or pride of ownership. I buy in at work for several reasons:

"One, my work is a personal reflection on me and my reputation; two, it reflects the quality of our organization and determines our status in the community. Lastly, I buy in because I don't want to let my team down. They count on me and I count on them. We mentally own our work and the quality, we buy in to being really good, and, as a result, we get lots of compliments." Pete listened intently and told Joe, "This stuff is new to me; it sort of makes sense. Can we talk more at lunch later today?"

Questions:

How did Joe explain buy-in to Pete?

How would you describe buy-in to Pete?

CHARACTER

Defined:

Who you are when no one is looking.

Amanda pruned the shrubs correctly even when no one was checking her work; she knew it was the right thing to do.

Quote:

"Goodness is about character—integrity, honesty, kindness, generosity, moral courage, and the like. More than anything else, it is about how we treat other people."—Dennis Prager, radio talk show host, author, and speaker

Story:

Amanda spotted an object underneath the bushes as she was pruning shrubs with her crew. She cautiously reached down to discover it was a purse, weathered and faded. Curious, she looked inside and saw several items you might expect to find in a lady's purse, but she also discovered a wallet with two credit cards, two gift cards for $100 and $500 in cash.

Her co-workers were watching and got excited; they asked what she was going to do with this newfound treasure and was she going to share any of it with them. Amanda didn't respond as she continued to search through the purse and discovered a driver's license. She closed the purse and secured it in the work truck.

Her co-workers were by this time getting more excited, talking about everything they would use the money for. Finally, one of them asked her, "What are you going to do with all that free money?" Without hesitation, Amanda replied, "I am going to see if we can find the owner of the purse and return it to her. That is what I would want someone to do for me."

Within a few days, Amanda had located the relieved owner of the purse and heard the story of how it had mysteriously disappeared one night after a ballgame some six months ago. Claude, who worked with Amanda, pulled her to the side and said, "That is why people respect you so much: you do the right thing, even when you could have easily kept all that money. We all know it was the right thing to do, but you actually did it. Thank you!"

Questions:

What do you think about Amanda's decision to find the owner of the purse?

Describe the type of character Amanda displayed in this story.

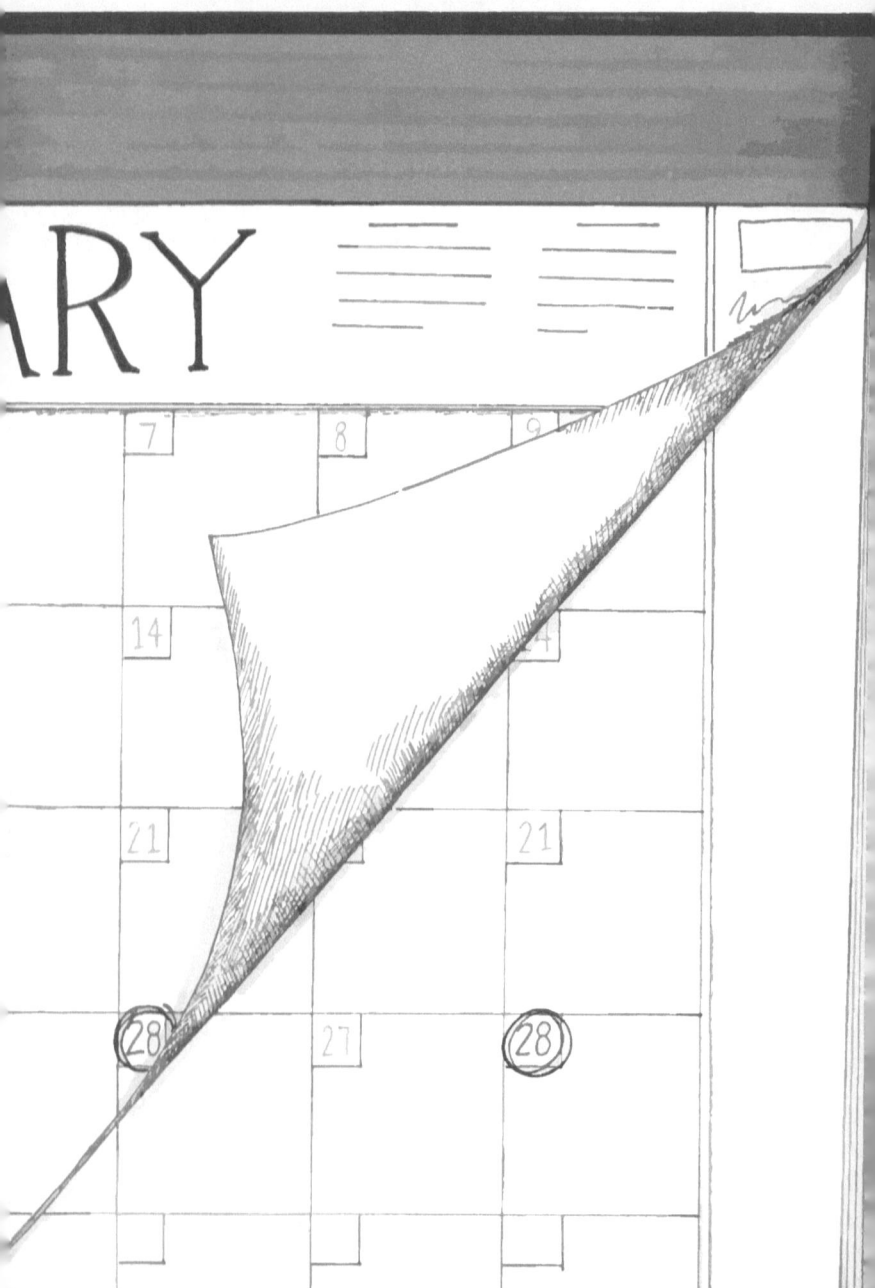

CIRCLE BACK

Defined:

To get back in touch, to let me know, to close the loop by communicating with the boss, the team, the customers, or others who need the information and updates.

Raymon started circling back with his boss to communicate updates and build a better working relationship.

Quote:

"My respect and trust grows for someone when they circle back with me with updates on a project, especially if they do it consistently."—Jeff McManus, leadership training author and speaker, and Ole Miss director of landscape services

Story:

Raymon was preoccupied at work when a serious mishap occurred. The next day, Clayton, the team supervisor, made sure to sit down and talk through with Raymon what had happened. Raymon had owned what went wrong and was able to share what he learned from the mistake. But because it was a serious mishap, Clayton needed to make sure Raymon was making good progress to correct the issue, so they set up a time to meet 30 days later, to circle back and discuss progress.

Setting up a time to circle back was a very good step, and Raymon was able to see the bigger picture of his actions. After the second meeting, Clayton wanted to set up another meeting to review the development and to keep building on the improvements.

This time, though, Raymon surprised Clayton by saying, "I need to show you I have grown in this process. I want to set up the meetings with you to circle back." Clayton agreed. So, over the next year, every 30 days, Raymon circled back with Clayton to provide updates and insights.

After a year, Clayton told Raymon, "You continue to show improvements in your decision-making, your attitude, and how you are helping others on our team. I wish the accident had never happened, but by constantly circling back and working to improve, you have turned that lemon into lemonade. Thank you for building the trust back into our working relationship."

Questions:

Why did Clayton want to circle back with Raymon after the mishap?

After Raymon had circled back with his supervisor for several months, what good came from the consistent communications?

COACHABLE

Defined:

Ready to listen, accept, and embrace feedback to improve.

Walter became a great team player after he became coachable and applied his supervisor's feedback daily.

Quote:

"My best skill was that I was coachable. I was a sponge and aggressive to learn."—Michael Jordan, Chicago Bulls forward regarded as the greatest basketball player of all time

Story:

Walter and Miles started work the same day. At first, both men struggled with getting to work on time, calling in sick, and having a grumpy attitude. Five years after their first day, Walter had advanced up several levels, while Miles was still in the same position he started in. Both men were similarly skilled and capable of doing the work. The difference? One word: coachability. Within their first three months on the job, each man took a very different attitude about work.

One day, Miles stopped Walter and asked why he was doing so much better than him in the company. "Surely you have friends in high places, or they like you better," Miles said. Walter was surprised by the question, but he thought for a second and said, "The difference in me and you are the decisions we made after the first three months here. I wanted to be a leader and make this a career, so I became very coachable. I worked on myself. At first, I was coming in late, calling in sick, being cranky and hard to work with, but I did like my job. That kept me employed, but it limited my opportunities to move up.

"Do you remember the day the boss talked to both of us and said if we wanted to excel here, we needed to listen and work to get better? At first, I thought he was nuts, but I tried it for 30 days and sure enough, he noticed and complimented me on the positive change. He asked us both to have a professional attitude and be positive with others, even when it was hard. After a year, you may remember, he gave us all a book to read. You said you didn't have time to read it, but I read it during my lunch breaks, and it helped me become a better team player.

The switch flipped for me and I worked on being coachable. Pretty soon, new opportunities opened up and I was promoted. "I encourage you to try it, Miles. Work on yourself, be coachable and you'll see a difference in the way people treat you and how opportunities show up."

Questions:

Why did Walter go higher in the company than Miles, even though they started work on the same day?

What does it mean to be coachable?

COMMITTED

Defined:

To be dedicated, loyal, and faithful.

Because John is committed to the new maintenance schedule, he believes it is the best way to proceed forward. Being committed means I care about creating quality results.

Quote:

"It was character that got us out of bed, commitment that moved us into action, and discipline that enabled us to follow through."—Zig Ziglar, personal development author and speaker

Story:

When Mary's team faced some criticism a few days ago, Mary asked her team members for ways they could learn to improve the quality of their work. Mary was concerned about the criticism but was very pleased to hear how many of her team members had ideas for improvement. A few of the ideas were used right away and others were discussed as possible solutions for the future. The team members discussed what they gained from the criticism.

One of the 15-year employees, Fred, was riding back to shop with Mary. Fred thanked her for asking for their input on how to deal with the criticism. "It made me feel motivated to be a part of the solution," Fred said. "You seemed to really want our input, and it gave me a deeper sense of commitment to our organization."

Mary nodded in agreement and added, "When I was just starting to work here, my boss taught me that if I wanted to get people to be committed and loyal to what we are doing, then I needed to treat them fairly and try to let them be a part of the solutions, whenever possible. Asking for everyone's input during the hard times helps validate that we value our team members, we appreciate them. I am committed to being a great organization with great people."

Questions:

How did Mary handle the criticism?

How did letting people give ideas on how to handle criticism help build a deeper level of commitment?

DEPENDABLE

Defined:

Trustworthy and reliable.

Melvin's reputation at work was that he was very reliable and dependable.

Quote:

"It's so simple really: If you say you're going to do something, do it. If you start something, finish it."—Epictetus, Greek Stoic philosopher

Story:

It was Melvin's last day of work, after thirty-five great years of dependable, loyal, and faithful service. A small crowd gathered for his retirement party, and when Melvin's boss stood up to speak, he gave everyone tremendous insights into what made Melvin so loved and so successful. "Melvin was not only here each day; he showed up early and was always ready at starting time. But that was just a small part of who Melvin was daily.

"Melvin has always been responsible with how he cares for the equipment, tools, and resources he uses each day. Over the years, Melvin earned the respect and trust of his fellow workers because you could depend on him, because his word was his bond. If he said the weeds were pulled, you could trust that the weeds were pulled and the job was done right. His positive attitude was contagious to others; with just his kind looks and agreeable manner, he influenced others to be positive, too. Melvin mentored many of you here today. He went the second mile by teaching you how to do pruning, mowing, mulching, and, most of all, how to do life. You know if he said it, you could depend on it."

The boss paused, looked Melvin in the eye, and said, "Melvin, you are leaving here today knowing you are respected because of your great work ethic, how you treated others, and your high-quality work. But most of all, you are leaving us all better because you taught us how to be dependable in having a good attitude, and through your willingness to go the extra mile and help others."

Questions:

What was Melvin's legacy at his workplace?

How did Melvin influence his workplace?

EXTRA MILE

Defined:

To give additional service when it is not expected.

Two new students asked Patrick how to get to the gym. He stopped mowing and walked them to the gym even though that was not his primary responsibility.

Quote:

"You can start right where you stand and apply the habit of going the extra mile by rendering more service and better service than you are now being paid for."—Napoleon Hill, author of *Think and Grow Rich*

Story:

Patrick was busy taking care of his daily mowing routine on the college campus where he worked. Two new students walking by stopped and asked him how to get to the gym. At first, he tried to explain how to get there, but reading their facial expressions, Patrick could see they were very confused. He smiled and said, "Follow me; I'll show you."

In a less than five minutes, he had walked the students to the gym and they were grateful. Patrick had gone the extra mile to help the students, then resumed his normal work schedule.

Questions:

How did Patrick go the extra mile when the students asked for directions?

What kind of impression do you think the girls had when Patrick went the extra mile to walk them to the gym?

EYE FOR DETAIL

Defined:

Paying attention to the little details that make the big picture.

Denny focused on the quality of his work by having an eye for detail on each job site.

Quote:

"It's attention to detail that makes the difference between average and stunning."—Francis Atterbury, English man of letters, politician, and bishop under Queen Anne

Story:

Denny was using his favorite line trimmer, the one that seems to be formed to his hands. As always, he made sure he trimmed the turfgrass at the same level as the mowers had cut. As he walked toward his next area to trim, he surveyed the surrounding area for any stray spurs of grass that the mowers may have missed so he could take care of them with his trimmer. He was using his eye for detail.

Denny looked at the new student worker he was coaching and said, "When we are using a line trimmer, it is important to always match the height of the mowers, so everything is even and consistent. Don't scalp the turf or trim it lower than the mowers are cutting. If you do, it looks unprofessional. If you see any little grass spurs or 'rooster tails' where the mowers may have accidently missed, trim those as you move to the next area."

Because Denny is so good at having an eye for detail and coaching others, the boss asked him to train new employees. "Make sure the line trimmer never scalps the turf," Denny tells the new workers. "If you cut too low and scalp the turf, it looks bad, and it allows weeds to germinate, which, over time, lowers the quality of the grass. When we display a good eye for detail, it gives our customers assurance that they can always trust us to do the job right. When they're satisfied with our quality, they'll tell their friends, and that means more work and more opportunity for all of us."

CULTIVATE

Questions:

What did Denny teach new workers about having an eye for detail?

According to Denny, why is scalping the turf grass a bad thing?

47

FOCUS

Defined:

To stay on target. Don't get distracted. To keep the main thing the main thing.

Quote:

"Your focus should be on creating an environment where growth can occur and then letting nature take its course."
—Patrick Lencioni, team management expert and author

Story:

It was a rainy day, but instead of staying home, Sharon's landscape crew had an opportunity to travel a couple hours and visit another landscape company. The owner of Sharon's company had arranged for the day trip so they could pick up new ideas. When Sharon's group arrived at Green Thumb Landscaping, they noticed right away how clean and organized the front of the building looked. It was an inviting and attractive entrance.

After Sharon's crew entered into the lobby, they were given a brief history and tour of the company. They observed inspiring photos, quotes all around the office, and emails from happy customers posted on a bulletin board. They were shown how Green Thumb brings new employees up to speed quickly and the classes they use to train staff. When they got to the area where the crew trucks were parked, they found a very organized place for all the equipment, visible labels indicating where tools belong, and even a plant identification station for employees to learn plant names.

"We emphasize growing our teams' knowledge and skills and becoming solution-motivated people," the tour guide explained. "Our focus is to help our customers, by developing and growing our employees. Several years ago, we saw how great companies outside our industry focused on developing their people. These companies experienced growth, great reviews, and more opportunities. Since we started developing our people five years ago, our company has gotten better clients and less employee turnover."

Sharon took lots of photos and notes, and was excited about all the new ideas she had seen. When she got back to her own office, the owner stuck his head in and asked what was her big take-away from visiting Green Thumb Landscaping. "Focus," she said. "They focus on servicing their customers by developing their people. Everything in the company is about learning, inspiring, and having a culture that focuses on growing great plants, employees, and customers." The owner smiled and said, "I thought you'd like what they are doing. Now, how do we implement what they are doing at our company?"

Questions:

What were some of things that Sharon saw Green Thumb Landscaping doing?

If you were Sharon, what would you recommend to the owner to help focus on growing their people?

HIGH STANDARDS

Defined:

Doing my work with exceptional quality.

Steven's team continues to get great ratings because they do a wonderful job meeting the high standards they set for each property.

Quote:

"Excellence is to do a common thing in an uncommon way."
—Booker T. Washington, American educator, author, and civil rights leader

Story:

"Hey, did we grab all the loose limbs we had stacked in the back?" Steven asked as he was about to drive away. "No, we can get them the next time we come by this way," said Rob, who had just started working for the company. Before Steven pulled off, he stopped and motioned for Rob to come help load the forgotten limbs.

"Why can't we just get these limbs next week?" Rob asked. "Why did we stop and get them now?" Steven answered, "Because we take a lot of pride in doing it the right way. This gives our customers a great experience with our company. If we leave the limbs here, the property looks unkept, sloppy, and unfinished. One of the reasons our customers choose us is because we have high standards about our work. They know our quality is exceptional."

Rob reflected briefly and said, "I get it: If we leave the limbs for next week, it looks like we didn't care and maybe the perception is that we lowered our standards." Pleased that Rob caught on so quickly, Steven said, "That's right, Rob, we are not like others; we want to meet our high standards every day."

Questions:

Why didn't Steven leave the limbs in the back to pick up next week?

What does Rob's comment mean? "If we leave the limbs for next week, it looks like we didn't care and maybe the perception is that we lowered our standards."

INITIATIVE

Defined:

Taking responsibility to get started, to ensure quality, being proactive.

On a rainy day, Sam took the initiative to use down time to clean the trucks and organize the storage shed.

Quote:

"Initiative is doing the right things without being told."—Elbert Hubbard, American writer, publisher, artist, and philosopher.

Story:

"Sam, I noticed you cleaned out the truck and organized the storage shed without being asked," said Ted, his boss. "You continue to add value to our organization by being helpful and assisting in areas that need attention. Where did you learn how to do this?"

"When I was playing sports in high school, I learned that if I only did what the coaches said, I would make them happy, but it didn't guarantee I could be the best," Sam explained. "I had to challenge myself, push harder, and outwork my competition. I guess that became who I am; I just like to take the initiative to do what needs to be done to help us be the best.

Jake, a coworker, overheard the conversation and began to snicker and roll his eyes. He had been working for years at the company and thought Sam was just trying to brown-nose the boss. He was very suspicious of Sam's behavior.

A few months passed, and Sam continued to show progress and growth in his work. He applied for and received a promotion to supervisor. Over the next year, Sam continued to take initiative to help his crew get better and become leaders in the organization. After watching Sam day in and day out, Jake began to believe Sam's proactive attitude was real. Jake found himself being challenged to be more proactive because of Sam. The two men became great leaders in the organization and helped create additional opportunities for employees to grow and expand their roles.

Questions:

How did Sam take initiative at the work place?

What did Jake think about Sam, both at first and then at the end of the story?

LEADING BY EXAMPLE

Defined:

A good role model, someone who takes initiative to do things with excellence.

Robert leads by example because he is trustworthy, is consistently dependable, and has a good attitude.

Quote:

"The single biggest way to impact an organization is to focus on leadership development. There is almost no limit to the potential of an organization that recruits good people, raises them up as leaders, and continually develops them."—John Maxwell, New York Times-bestselling leadership author and minister

Story:

Robert was promoted to president of a company that managed a large property. Each morning, he had a habit of walking the property, picking up litter and even pulling weeds from the flower beds. Robert's role was administrative; he worked with lawyers, accountants, and other administrators, generally staying in his office most of the day. He spent hours raising money and building relationships to grow the company's assets. He was not a landscaper.

Even after many years as the leader, Robert continued to interact with the 3,000 or so company employees, spontaneously stopping by to say hello, shake hands, and interact with workers at all levels. One day, one of the landscapers asked his boss, "Why does our president, Mr. Robert, walk the campus and pick up litter every day? It seems like he has so many other things to do with his time; that seems menial for him to do."

The boss replied, "He cares. He is not afraid to do the little things; he's leading by example. He knows if he does it, he sets the right example for all of us to follow. His passion for the property is reflected by his actions." The landscaper nodded and said, "I don't even really know Robert, but I respect him. He's not afraid to get his hands dirty. I like that."

Questions:

What did Robert do to lead by example?

How did leading by example make the landscaper respect Robert?

MOMENTUM

Defined:

The multiplied energy behind teamwork when combined with preparation, focus, and action to accomplish a great task or vision.

Cliff knew if his team came together and focused on their goals, they could gain great momentum from accomplishing their project.

Quote:

"Momentum is whatever your attitude determines it to be."
—Lou Holtz, College Football Hall of Fame coach and network analyst

Story:

It had been a long day; the crew had been mulching leaves and working hard to beat an incoming storm. They had covered a lot of ground, even with two employees out sick. When Cliff reached his team, he was amazed at the progress, energy, and drive of the entire team. He grabbed a backpack and starting dusting off areas as the crew progressed through the leaves. After about an hour, they were finished. They paused for a minute to look at all they had accomplished and to enjoy the feeling you get when you finish a big job.

As everyone was taking it all in, Cliff asked, "How did you guys get so much completed today? You were down two workers, yet you didn't get behind; you actually were ahead of schedule. How?" Perry, a mower operator, spoke up and said, "I guess we had momentum on our side. Everybody here knew what we had to do and the high standards we each expected. We knew that tomorrow, we wouldn't get a second chance to do these leaves. This morning, before we started work, we came together and devised a plan to win the day and discussed the challenges we might face.

"Each person added insights to the plan, then each person took on a role they would do. We all had the general understanding that there was no standing around and we needed to get creative to get finished before the rain came. It wasn't perfect—one blower went down, and we had a flat on one of the mulching mowers. We adapted, we overcame, and we won the day." Cliff was excited and agreed, "You sure did win the day. Thank you everyone!"

Questions:

What are some of the things that contributed to Cliff's team getting momentum?

What were some of the obstacles the team had to overcome to win the day?

OWNERSHIP

Defined:

Ownership is when I take full responsibility for a job.

Rocio took ownership in his pruning by taking pride in his work.

Quote:

"The work each person produces on the outside is a reflection of who they are on the inside."—Matt Hogan, master martial arts instructor and founder of MoveMe Quotes

Story:

Rocio welcomed a new landscape employee, Max, to his crew. Later, as the two were working together, Rocio looked Max in the eye and said, "I want you to have ownership in the way your turf, shrubs, and trees look. I want you to treat each location, each seasonal color bed, each piece of equipment like it is your own." Max looked confused at first, but listened in hopes he would understand the concept. He asked, "You want me take ownership in each lawn, just like it is my own yard?"

"Absolutely," Rocio agreed. "We all take ownership in our work and it reflects a high level of quality work. Everything we do reflects on us, our team, and our company. We care about how the areas we maintain look, and we stake our name on it. We also take care of our equipment, check the fluids, keep blades sharp, and always put tools back where they go at the end of the day. It is the little things—like taking ownership in all the aspects of our day—that makes us a leader in our industry. And when you're the leader, you have opportunities to grow."

Max was puzzled, but pleased as he explained to Rocio, "I don't know if I can do this ownership thing. This is very new to me. I'm pretty nervous because I've never worked where this was taught." Rocio reassured him, saying, "Don't worry, Max, you will get the feel for ownership as you get more confident in your work. As for now, keep being coachable, and I will help you be successful."

Questions:

How did Rocio explain what ownership is to Max?

Max was nervous about taking ownership; how would you coach him to take ownership of his work?

PREPARED

Defined:

To be organized, to equip, to plan, and to get ready.

Javier prepared for the next day by setting out his clothes the night before, so he could quickly get dressed in the morning.

Quote:

"You were born to win, but to be a winner, you must plan to win, prepare to win, and expect to win."—Zig Ziglar, personal development author and speaker

Story:

Farmer Boyd looked over his field full of ripe vegetables and watched the rain bathe the produce one last time before his team went in to harvest it, hopefully tomorrow. He turned around when he heard Javier driving the four-wheeler through the mud next to the barn, stopping nearby.

"I guess we should go home since it's raining; maybe we can work tomorrow," Javier suggested. Farmer Boyd grinned and said, "Javier, you're new to the farm, so I want you learn a valuable life lesson today. Take a quick look at everyone who works for me right now and what do you see them doing?"

For the first time that day, Javier noticed his fellow workers. "It looks like those two guys at the trucks are changing the oil filters and servicing the trucks." Then he pointed, "Bonnie has all the lights on in the combine and is changing out the burned-out bulbs, while Jimmy over there has a can of lubricant spraying down all the padlocks and door hinges. It looks like Oscar is repairing a tire. Right here at this tractor, I can see Dustin is greasing it."

Farmer Boyd replied, "That's good, Javier, you see everyone is getting ready for the harvest that starts as soon as the weather is dry enough, hopefully tomorrow." Hoping Javier would see the value of being prepared, Farmer Boyd asked, "Javier, if we go home and don't get prepared, what do you think could happen once we start harvesting?" Javier grinned and replied, "I guess we run the risk of having equipment break down and having to stop and do repairs. That would delay our work and cost more to repair then."

Farmer Boyd was pleased to hear how much Javier understood the value of being prepared. "OK, I get it," Javier said. "What do you need me to do to prepare for success tomorrow?"

Questions:

How did Farmer Boyd teach Javier about how to prepare for the harvest?

What are things we do today to prepare for tomorrow's work?

PROBLEM SOLVER

Defined:

A person who is solution-focused.

Jim empowered his team to be problem solvers by training and equipping them.

Quote:

"Most people spend more time and energy going around problems than in trying to solve them. If you always do what you've always done, you'll always get what you've always got."—Henry Ford, founder of Ford Motor Co.

Story:

When Jim and his crews came to work one morning, heavy overnight rains had eroded a steep hillside behind the maintenance shop right into their equipment area. Sand and red mud covered the parking lot, as well as underneath their trucks and mowers. As workers tiptoed through the mud to reach their equipment, they tracked mud around the compound and into the trucks, restrooms, and offices. It was an overall unpleasant situation.

At three levels of the organization, people jumped in to solve this major erosion problem. The crews needed to get out to work quickly, so employees worked fast to find temporary solutions to deal with the mess. They broke down empty cardboard boxes and used them as temporary bridges across the mud. This allowed them to load and leave the shop area.

Supervisors gathered for a quick stand-up meeting to determine the best way to remove the mud from the around the shop. After the crews headed out, two supervisors quickly got a skid loader and backhoe together to scoop up the mud. In less than 30 minutes, they cleared most of mess and used high-pressure hoses to wash down the area.

Meanwhile, Jim was on the phone with the owner of the property next door, from where the mud came. A few minutes later, Jim asked his designer to develop a plan to mitigate the problem permanently. Within a couple days, the owner next door had hired Jim's company to fix the slope with rock-lined ditches channeling water down the hill, adding new vegetation to hold the topsoil and plenty of fresh mulch.

Questions:

How did this organization deal with the erosion, both short-term and long-term?

Why didn't Jim and his company ignore the mud problem and just go do their work?

PROFESSIONALISM

Defined:

A professional is proficient, an expert, someone who conducts himself or herself with integrity and the highest respect for others, the equipment, and the property.

Miguel was complimented on his courteous behavior and his neat appearance as he worked in the park; he was a true professional.

Quote:

"Professional is not a label you give yourself; it's a description you hope others will apply to you."—David Maister, Harvard Business School professor and author

Story:

Each time a group of people walks in front of Miguel, he steps aside, throttles down the blower, and lets them pass by on the sidewalk. Although he is expected to get his work done quickly, Miguel also knows he has to be professional about how he conducts himself on the job. He understands that people walking and enjoying the park are the priority, so he is always respectful by lowering his blower, making eye contact, nodding and smiling to acknowledge their presence.

He learned quickly on this job not to make people feel uncomfortable by staring or holding eye contact too long. He was shocked one day to see another worker stare at a group of joggers and then whistle at them. Miguel knew that behavior was out of line and unprofessional, and that worker received several complaints about his immature behavior.

As a professional, Miguel knows his job and performs it with excellence. He also takes great pride in how he presents himself each day, always making sure his uniform is clean and taking care of his personal grooming to show he understands what it means to have a professional appearance. Because Miguel sees himself and acts as a professional, others are more likely to treat him that way.

Questions:

How did Miguel demonstrate that he is a professional?

How does being a professional help us at work?

RELATIONAL

Defined:

Being relational is working with people.

Angelo mowed lawns daily, but he knew it was important to talk with customers and have good chemistry with co-workers; he was very respectful, no matter the situation.

Quote:

"You can make more friends in two months by becoming interested in other people than you can in two years by trying to get other people interested in you."—Dale Carnegie, lecturer, self-improvement expert, and author of *How to Win Friends and Influence People*

Story:

"Hey Angelo, why are we doing this leadership class with my crew today when we have lots of work to do outside?" Robb asked. Angelo thought it was a good question, so he answered, "One of the things that makes our company uniquely different is we take the time to invest in building our workers. If we focus only on developing skills like mowing, edging, and pruning, we miss the opportunity to become better people and better team players and, ultimately, creating the award-winning results we're known for."

"Hey, you're right," Robb said. "This course has helped me become a better leader at work and a better person. I can tell our crew does not have a lot of drama, and we are working like a real team. Having us do this class each month has made a huge difference in the way we communicate and collaborate, and it's given us a positive attitude.

"Last week, one of my worst team members asked how he could become a better team player. He's become coachable and has taken on more responsibility. Angelo, you've really helped make us better by taking the time to improve the way we work together. Thank you for helping me see how important it is to be relational and invest in our people."

Questions:

How was Angelo helping Robb do his work better?

How did Robb see a difference in his crew when they took a course on leadership together?

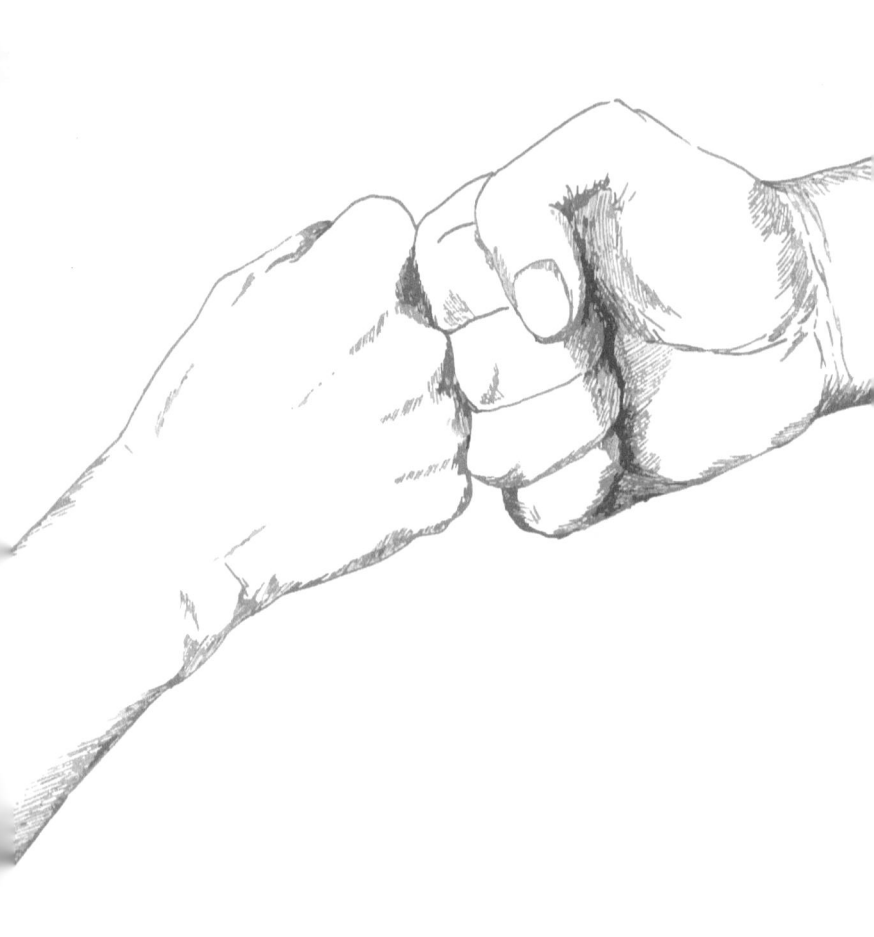

RESPECT

Defined:

To value one's self and others.

A.J. modeled respect by being at work five minutes early each day and showing high regard for his teammates.

Quote:

"Respect yourself and those you work with."—John Maxwell, New York Times-bestselling leadership author and minister

Story:

A.J. asked his coworker Josh, "Why do you give so much of your time to help me get my work right? I have never worked in a place where people help each other like this. You give me the credit for work you've helped me do. Why is that, Josh?"

Josh never stopped working as he answered. "It's because I do want you, our customers, and our company to be successful," he said. "A.J., the work you do is important; no matter what it is, it is needed and valued. It may not seem important at the time, but if you do it wrong, slow or not at all, it shows a lack of respect for yourself. Your co-workers will notice how you have disrespected yourself and they may lose respect for you, too. Never think of what you do as just manual labor; it's not. Our results inspire and motivate others every day.

"Second, respect and value those around you, because what they do is important too. We work as a team to create and maintain a masterpiece in the landscape. If we let our egos get in the way and we want all the credit or we look down on our co-workers, it causes our quality of work to drop, and this can cause tension on our team. We build team respect by working together in harmony. We earn and show respect by doing a really great job."

A.J. nodded and said, "That makes sense, but it does challenge me, Josh. I have to respect myself and my teammates by having pride in what I do. Thanks for coaching me and helping me to understand that."

Questions:

How does Josh show respect to A.J.?

Why did Josh tell A.J. that the work he did is significant?

REWARD

Defined:

Bigger than any payment, the internal satisfaction of a job well done.

Charles had a sense of real satisfaction and pride as he finished trimming the last of the oak trees at the front entrance.

Quote:

"Success is not the key to happiness. Happiness is the key to success. If you love what you are doing, you will be successful."—Herman Cain, American businessman and presidential candidate, former chairman of the Federal Reserve Bank of Kansas City

Story:

When Charles was a boy, his father taught him that hard work would provide a steady paycheck, but if he did the work well and with pride, it would provide him with something much more valuable. Charles' dad called it the reward: that feeling inside of doing a job right, making sure you put your best into it. "That internal reward you get from doing your best is what keeps you liking your work," his dad said. "It helps fuel the passion to be the best."

Charles explained it to a coworker he was mentoring: "In landscaping, we get the reward by turning an ugly property into a beautiful one, or by mowing turf properly so it looks perfectly manicured. It is a satisfying feeling when we do it right, and others enjoy what we have produced. It's not all about the money at work, and it's not even about getting the praise and recognition; it's about the satisfaction we get for a job well done."

Questions:

How does Charles describe a reward?

How does personal pride fit in to our work according to Charles?

SELF-IMPROVEMENT

Defined:

Taking the initiative to work to better yourself.

Joseph was learning to speak Spanish as a step in self-improvement.

Quote:

"Work on yourself more than you do on your job."—Jim Rohn, entrepreneur, author, and motivational speaker

Story:

Joseph asked his team to meet at his truck's tailgate before everyone starting working. "Today, I want to share something with all of you to help you be successful in life," he said. "You will have more opportunities to move up in life if you do this one thing. If you'll focus on this one item, you can improve your work life and your home life." Pedro shouted out, "Tell us, what is the one thing we need to do?" Joseph smiled and replied, "Self-improvement." A hush came over the group.

Joseph looked Pedro in the eye and said, "If you will work on *yourself* every day, new opportunities will open up. For a long time, I just kept thinking that if everyone else would change, my job would be better. But then, I heard a guy speak, and he challenged me to work on improving myself first. I was skeptical, but then I started looking for ways to be a better leader. I wanted to stop getting mad when people didn't meet my expectations, and I wanted to stop complaining and being negative. So, I took a leadership course online at night. It really helped me. I didn't get upset as easy and I became a better person. This year, I am learning to speak Spanish, so I took a Spanish class online during lunch."

"We noticed you had changed," Pedro said. "You are listening to us and working to make us a team." Joseph was excited to hear his efforts were being appreciated. "Thanks for noticing, Pedro," he said. "I wanted to share this with all of you because self-improvement has made me a better person and us a better team."

Questions:

What did Joseph learn about self-improvement?

What are five different ways someone can improve themselves, both personally and at work?

SELF-STARTER

Defined:

A person who has the initiative and drive to get results.

Brad gained a competitive advantage by looking for a job even in places that were not posting job openings.

Quote:

"Successful people don't have fewer problems. They have determined that nothing will stop them from going forward."—Ben Carson, neurosurgeon, author, and U.S. Secretary of Housing and Urban Development

Story:

The afternoon after being laid off due to COVID-19, Brad scoured the internet for a new job. He applied for several and posted his resume. Then he looked on a map and found ten places he thought he might enjoy working and went out to visit each one. Asking to see the manager or owner each time, he looked them in the eye and let them know he saw their business as a potential great place to work. "I know you may not be hiring today, but you will one day, and I wanted to let you know I would be interested in interviewing," he said. "Here is my resume. I'm a self-starter and I invite you to contact my former boss and ask him about my work habits."

Within two days, Brad had six job interviews lined up and four days later, he had three offers, all paying more than his last position. About two months into his new job, Brad asked the owner, "Why did you hire me?" The owner replied, "Two reasons: I called your former boss, and he said you're a self-starter and that he would hire you back if the company hadn't closed down. Second, the day you stopped by, you showed me something about yourself that I admired." Brad asked, "What, was it my resume?"

"No, your resume was good, but I see good resumes all the time," his boss explained. "It was the proactive way you were looking for work. By not waiting around or relying on a job to be posted, you showed you had energy and willingness to do what others wouldn't do. And now that you've been working here, I can see that I was right; you're self-motivated and a self-starter. Each day, you look for jobs around here to do; you don't wait to be told what to do. You are constantly adding value. You ask questions to learn, and I see you reading about plants to learn their names and become better at work. Self-starters don't wait to be told; they do it, and that is you, Brad."

Questions:

What did Brad do as a self-starter to get hired and to get better at work?

What made Brad the perfect choice for his new job?

SELFLESS

Defined:

To put the needs of others above myself.

Xavier was selfless because he used his own personal time to help co-workers learn their plant names, so they could pass the plant identification exam.

Quote:

"It is amazing what you can accomplish if you do not care who gets the credit."—Harry S. Truman, 33rd president of the United States

Story:

After five long years, Xavier's dream of becoming team leader was finally happening. His boss was retiring in a month, but first he was spending time coaching, mentoring, and counseling Xavier to become a better person and leader. At times, Xavier's rough edges seemed to be in conflict with his team. He had to learn to value people and believe in them. When the company's owner made the official announcement about Xavier's new promotion, he asked Xavier if he wanted to say a few words to his new team.

Xavier nodded yes, but his emotions over took for a moment as he paused to collect his thoughts. Taking a deep breath, Xavier said, "When I came to work here five years ago, I was not ready to be a leader. I was an arrogant and conceited know-it-all. My attitude wasn't right because I didn't realize how much I didn't know about working with others. I wasn't investing in people and I didn't appreciate all the work the team does. As you know, our wonderful boss is retiring next month. I would not be standing here in this position if it were not for him being selfless by investing his time in me. He coached me, helped me see my blind spots, and got me to see the value of believing in my team. I will always be grateful to him for his selfless actions of investing and supporting me."

With that, Xavier stopped, walked over and shook his old boss' hand and said, "Thank you for being selfless by investing in me, even when you didn't have to."

Questions:

How did Xavier's boss change the course of Xavier's career and life?

How was Xavier's boss being selfless?

THANKFUL

Defined:

To be appreciative. To be grateful.

Ronnie was thankful he was able to work and provide for his family.

Quote:

"No matter what our circumstance, we can find a reason to be thankful."—David Jeremiah, author, pastor, and founder of Turning Point Radio and Television Ministries

Story:

Ronnie, one of the most dependable longtime employees, had been out on medical leave and returned just a few days ago. As the crew was about to break their morning huddle, Ronnie asked if he could say a few words. "Of course, Ronnie; go ahead," his supervisor said as he put his clipboard aside.

"Guys, most of you know I have been fighting some tough stuff with my old body," Ronnie began. "It's been a long road, but I want you to know I would not trade any of it for the world." Several of his teammates looked confused. "I have learned to be thankful for what I have: a good life, a good team, and another chance to be alive," he continued. "I am grateful that I have the opportunity to work with my hands, help create beautiful landscapes for people to enjoy, and most of all, to be around you all." The team encouraged Ronnie, and a few patted him on the back and said they were glad he was back.

As the huddle broke, one the younger guys stopped Ronnie and asked, "Did you really mean it when you said you wouldn't trade being sick?" Ronnie looked him in the eye and said, "Yes, it took getting sick for me to realize how much I already have. I was constantly wanting more and more and never was happy, but this trial showed me that God has already blessed me so much. I just need to recognize what He has given me." The young man smiled and said, "Thanks for sharing that. I know exactly what you mean about always wanting more and more and not being happy. That makes me want to focus on the right things, and I need to take your approach of gratitude for what

I have. Thank you for sharing this morning, Ronnie, you have given me a better direction to live my life."

Questions:

Why was Ronnie thankful even after being out on medical leave?

What was the young man who spoke to Ronnie struggling with?

TOUGHNESS

Defined:

To be persistent, determined, tenacious; to have grit.

Fernando showed his toughness in buying his first home by working long hours. He kept going, even when he wanted to quit, and overcame a big learning curve.

Quote:

"You just can't beat the person who won't give up."—Babe Ruth, Hall of Fame outfielder and slugger for the New York Yankees

Story:

"Never give up," Fernando's mom yelled as he headed out the front door. Just for a minute, Fernando wished she would stop saying that. After all, he was 29, had a family, and was trying to buy his first house. Life had not been easy since his dad died some twenty-five years ago. His mother worked three jobs when he was growing up, and he started selling newspapers at an early age to help make ends meet. Now, the mortgage company was asking for things he had never heard of. It was overwhelming; he almost wanted to quit and just go back to renting. But something inside kept him going.

Each time he came to an obstacle, he looked for ways to push through it. "Never give up," he would think. Sometimes that meant calling his cousin for help. The day finally came to close on the new house and get the keys, but first, he had to meet with the lawyers to sign lots of papers. It was intimidating and made him feel anxious, but Fernando kept hearing his mother's words, "Never give up." An hour later, he walked out of the office with the keys to his new house.

His cousin smiled and shook his hand, saying, "Congratulations on your new home, cuz. You've got the mental toughness to get through that challenging process. What kept you going?" Fernando breathed a sigh of relief and said, "I've always wanted my own home for my family. There were times I wanted to quit saving money, quit looking for houses, and quit the entire process. But Mom taught me to stay with it, and she always believed in me. That's what kept me going: her belief in me to 'never give up.'"

Questions:

How did Fernando display mental toughness in buying his house?

What role did his mother play in helping him?

TRUST

Defined:

Other's confidence in me; that I am honest, based on the integrity of my words and actions.

Mason trusted his team to get the job completed when he had to leave work for a week.

Quote:

"The glue that holds all relationships together—including the relationship between the leader and the led—is trust, and trust is based on integrity."—Brian Tracy, motivational speaker and self-help author

Story:

Mason believes that leading by example is the key to success for his crew and for the organization. He had been working on the park maintenance crew for just over two years when he was asked to lead a special project, with the possibility of moving to a new leadership level. At first, Mason was nervous about the new role, but he quickly showed he had what it takes to lead; he had gained the trust of his bosses and was promoted to supervisor.

Unfortunately, after about three years, Mason had grown a little sluggish and was constantly making slip-ups with employees and customers. He no longer practiced leading by example and seemed to have lost his drive for quality.

After several poor performance reviews and multiple counselings, Mason no longer had the trust of his bosses or his own crew, and he lost his supervisor position. At first, he tried to deflect the poor behavior on others, but he caught himself, knowing that he was ultimately responsible, and accepted the change.

Two years later, Mason was doing well in his new position. He had more accountability and contact with his boss, which helped him tremendously. He never became supervisor again, but he did become a vital team member who helped younger workers learn to flourish. He had rebuilt the trust to be a mentor to the younger staff members. In this role, Mason often told new employees, "Trust is hard to earn, but easy to lose. It takes years to build trust and just minutes to lose it. Be trustworthy even when no one is watching you."

Questions:

How did Mason gain and lose the trust of his bosses and crew?

Why was trust so important on Mason's team?

WALKING WITH WINNERS

Defined:

Carefully choosing who influences us daily.

Carmen listened to positive podcasts and read biographies of successful people to develop the mental mindset of a winner.

Quote:

"You are the average of the five people you spend the most time with."—Jim Rohn, entrepreneur, author, and motivational speaker

Story:

"Congratulations for leading your team to win another national award for the most beautiful landscape this year, Carmen," said Matt, a consultant for the organization. "The landscaping looks amazing. I remember when you first came, the landscape team was very disorganized, unmotivated, and indifferent about their jobs. No one really liked working here, and most of the employees didn't really care about the quality of their work, but somehow you changed all that. Today, your team is known as landscape national champions. How did you do it, Carmen; how did you get championship results with the same people who once didn't care?"

Carmen knew that Matt was serious, so he thought carefully before answering. "There were many things we changed, but one of the most important changes was that we started walking with winners," Carmen explained. "Winners want to win. They learn how to win and repeat those things. They don't make excuses; they take personal responsibility and they do what is needed to win the right way. When you work next to people who want to be winners, you either start working to win yourself, or you find somewhere else to work. Over time, our team's mindset changed from whiners to winners.

"Who you hang out with matters, and that's why we spend time at work being influenced by great teachers like John Maxwell, Jim Rohn, Les Brown, Zig Ziglar, Dave Ramsey, Tony Dungy, and others. How we think is how we will respond. Winners look at obstacles as minor setbacks to overcome. Whiners look at obstacles as an excuse to stop trying. Our national championships started coming when we started walking with winners and changed the way we saw ourselves."

Questions:

How did Carmen change the organization's mindset from losing to winning?

Why is it important is it to have positive influences in your life?

WORK SMARTER, NOT HARDER

Defined:

Doing projects efficiently; thinking ahead to eliminate cost and waste, and reduce labor.

Gary was working smarter, not harder, when he used the wheelbarrow to haul all the supplies to the backyard in one trip.

Quote:

"Lost time is never found again."—Benjamin Franklin, writer, statesman, diplomat, scientist, and a Founding Father of the United States

Story:

Gary moved the wheelbarrow six feet closer to where he and Leon were excavating for a drain. "Why did you do that?" Leon asked. "We can just throw the dirt over into the wheelbarrow from here."

Gary nodded and said, "Yes, we can do it the hard way or the more efficient way. If we throw it over to the wheelbarrow and miss, that means we have to eventually clean it up, and that takes more time to complete the job. When we throw the soil, we both get tired quicker.

"When we look for ways to save time and energy, it allows us to work smarter, not harder. Being efficient reduces our cost and allows us to keep the job in budget and stay in business. The customer is happy, we are happy, and our bosses are happy."

Questions:

Why did Gary move the wheelbarrow closer to where they were excavating?

How have you seen someone work smarter, not harder?

ACKNOWLEDGEMENT

This book had some great input from a lot of people. I want to thank my family—Suzanne, Sam, Nate, Josh, Ashley, Mark, and Jordan—for their continued support and input on this book. Thank you for my editor, Mitchell Diggs, who made great suggestions, edits, and tried to capture my ideas better than I could say it myself. Thank you to JoAnn Edwards for her continual input, edits, and meeting short deadlines. Thank you to Terri Shrader for your consistent and amazing work at The Jeff McManus Group, LLC.

Several people in the landscape industry have really cheered me on and added ideas and encouraged me to finish this book. Thank you to Tony Gibson, Kevin Mercier, Jerry Dobbs, Angelo Azevedo, Stephanie Bruno, Dean Hansen, Nathan Lazinksky, Tom Dickerson, Sam Johnson, Shea Baird, Steven Boatwright, Steven Murphy, Amanda Klenke, and Bonnie Black. Thank you for your input and encouragement on this project. All the stories are fiction, but many are based on true stories. All the names have been changed.

I owe Mark Ross, RLA, MBA, CPLC, ACC, and retired assistant parks and recreation director for all of Houston, Texas, a debt of gratitude. His input improved my focus and resilience on this book project. Those of you who wear many hats in life know how valuable a person like Mark can be.

Thank you, Beth Robinson, for all the amazing illustrations. Well done. Thank you for DeShone Thompson and Javier Sanchez for the being on the cover of this book. A big thanks to Mallory McManus of Mvisuals.info for the cover photo.

ABOUT THE AUTHOR

Jeff McManus is a member of the National Speakers Association and the author of *Growing Weeders into Leaders* and *Pruning Like a Pro*. Jeff works at the University of Mississippi as the landscape leader. Jeff developed systems of training and rewarding that he teaches to organizations. In his spare time, he works with leaders to cultivate their organization's growth and competitive advantage. That's why Forbes Magazine, The New York Times, USA Today, Facilities Executive, Huffington Post, Sports Field Turf, and others have cited Jeff's work. If you're looking to get inspired and inspire those around you, Jeff is a natural choice for your next speaking, training, or retreat. Visit www.jeffmcmanus.com now to connect.

READY FOR THE NEXT STEP?

Learn to cultivate your team culture and have your
team fully engaged with these fine videos.

https://jeffmcmanus.thinkific.com/

Does your organization or association need
a speaker for your next event?

Check availability now by emailing Jeff@Jeffmcmanus.com.